EDITION PETERS REPERTOIRE LIBRARY

English Songs
of the 17th and 18th centuries

Medium-low voice

PETERS EDITION LTD
A member of the EDITION PETERS GROUP
LEIPZIG · LONDON · NEW YORK

Also available from the
Edition Peters Repertoire Library (Voice)

English Songs of the 17th and 18th Centuries (*High voice*)
EP 72528 ISMN 979-0-57700-778-6

German Lieder of the 19th Century (*High voice*)
EP 72530 ISMN 979-0-57700-780-9

German Lieder of the 19th Century (*Medium-low voice*)
EP 72531 ISMN 979-0-57700-781-6

Works from this edition are drawn from the comprehensive Edition Peters vocal catalogue including *The Art of Song*, a graded series with selected repertoire from the Associated Board of the Royal Schools of Music singing syllabus.

Peters Edition Ltd
2–6 Baches Street
London
N1 6DN

Tel: +44 (0)20 7553 4000
Fax: +44 (0)20 7490 4921
Email: sales@editionpeters.com
Internet: www.editionpeters.com

Cover design: www.adamhaystudio.com

Printed in England by Halstan & Co, Amersham, Bucks.

CONTENTS

When daisies pied

range: 

William Shakespeare (1564–1616)

Thomas Arne (1710–1778)

[Allegretto]

5

1. When dai - sies pied and
shep - herds pipe on

10

vio - lets blue, And la - dy-smocks all sil - ver‿white, and cu-ckoo buds of
oat - en straw, And mer - ry larks are plough-men's clocks, and tur-tles tread, And

14

yel - low hue Do paint the mea - dows with‿ de - light;
rooks‿ and daws, And maid - ens bleach their sum - mer smocks.

18

The cu-ckoo then, on ev' - ry tree Mocks mar-ried men,

22
mocks mar-ried men, mocks mar-ried men; for thus sings he: Cu-ckoo, cu-ckoo,
27
cu-ckoo, cu-ckoo, cu-ckoo, cu-ckoo; O word of fear,
33
O word of fear, un - pleas - ing to a mar - ried ear, un - pleas - ing to a
38
1.
2.
mar - ried ear! 2. When ear!
43

Where the bee sucks

range: 

William Shakespeare (1564–1616)

Thomas Arne (1710–1778)

17
couch when owls do cry, when owls do cry, when owls do cry. On a
21
bat's back do I fly, do I fly, Af - ter
25
sun - set, mer-ri - ly, mer-ri - ly, Af - ter sun - set, mer - ri - ly.
1.
28a
2.
- ly.

32
Mer-ri - ly, mer-ri - ly shall I live now, Un - der the

36
blos-som that hangs on the bough, Mer-ri - ly, mer-ri - ly shall I live now, Un - der the

40
blos-som that hangs on the bough, Un - der the blos-som that hangs on the bough.

44

range: 

My lovely Celia

George Munro (?–1731) George Munro (?–1731)

My love - ly Ce - lia,
me Am - bro - sia
let me gaze

heav'n - ly fair, As lil - lies sweet, as soft as
in a kiss, That I may ri - val love in
on your bright eyes, Where melt - ing beams so oft a -

air, No more then tor - ment me, but be kind, And
bliss, That I may mix my soul with thine, And
- rise; My heart's en - chant - ed with thy charms. O,

1.2. 3.

with thy love ease my trou - bled mind. 2. Give
make the plea - sure all di - vine. 3. O,
take me, dy - ing to your arms.

Oft have I sigh'd

Thomas Campion (1567–1620)

Thomas Campion (1567–1620)

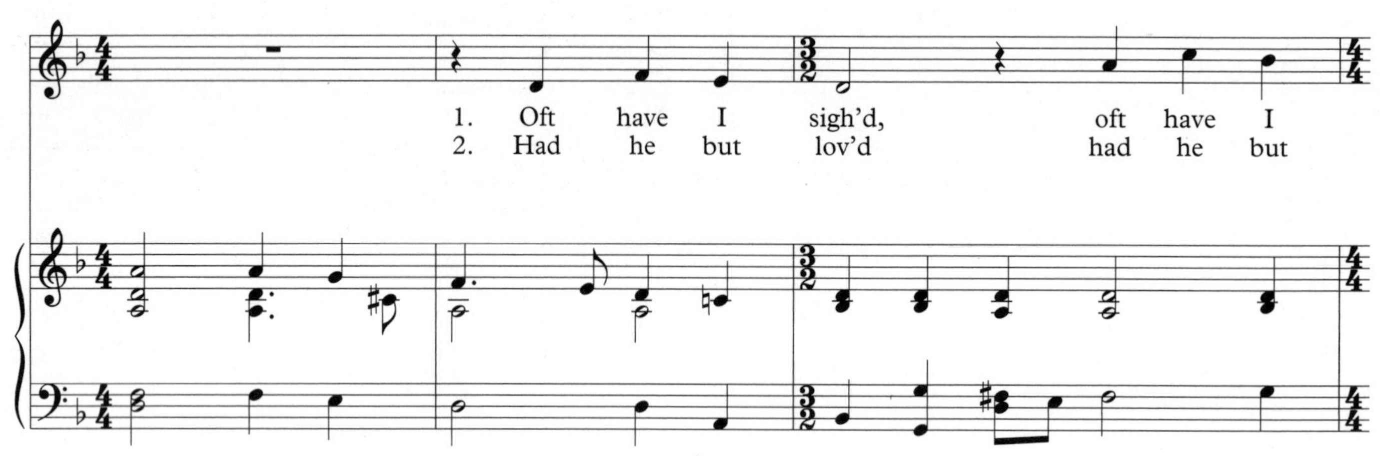

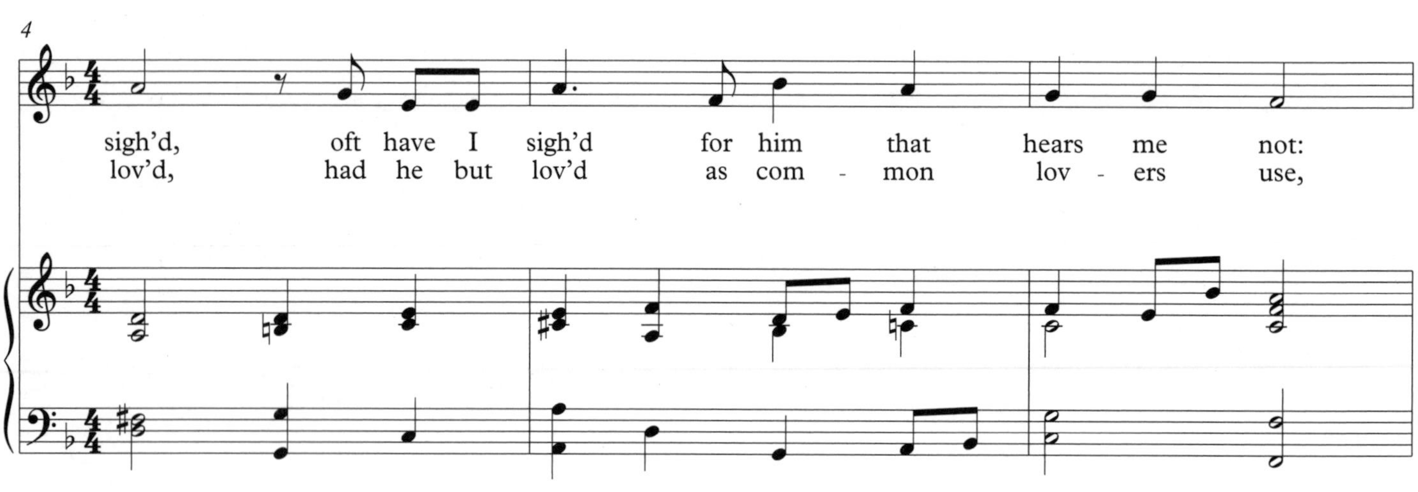

10
O ______ yet I lan - guish still, yet I lan - guish
O ______ yet I lan - guish still, yet I lan - guish

12
still, yet I lan - guish still through his de -
still, yet I lan - guish still, still con - stant

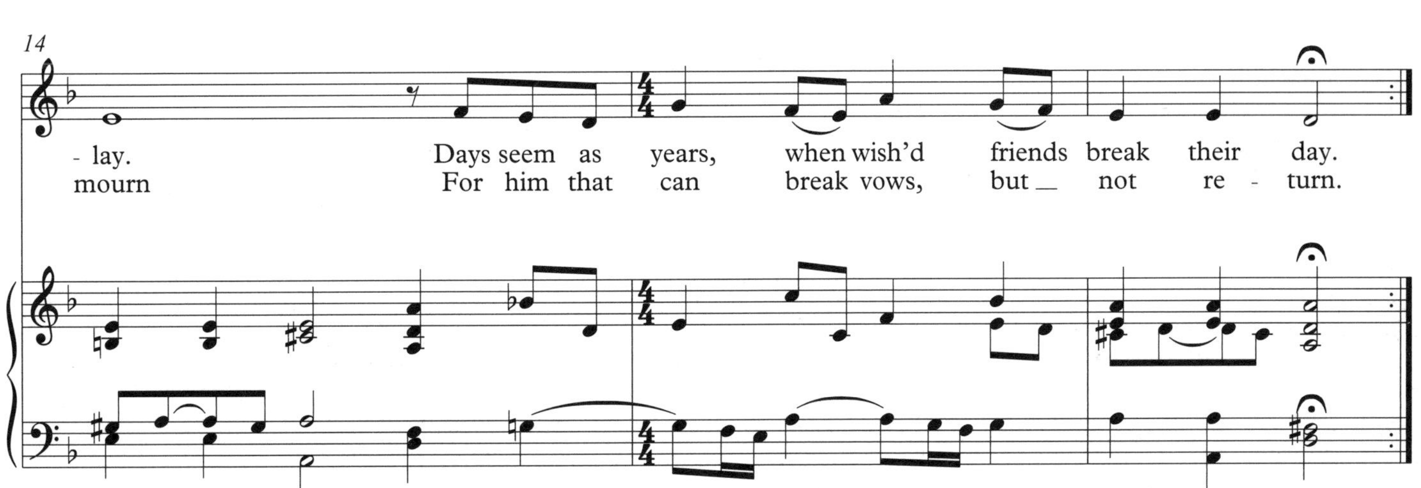
14
- lay. Days seem as years, when wish'd friends break their day.
mourn For him that can break vows, but _ not re - turn.

The peaceful western wind

range: 

Thomas Campion (1567–1620)

Thomas Campion (1567–1620)

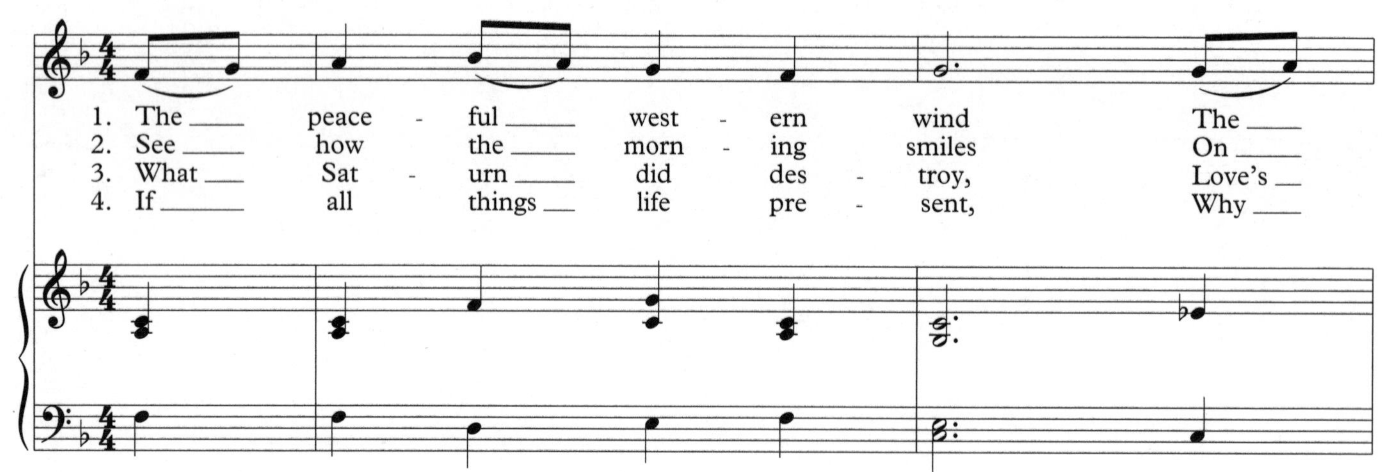

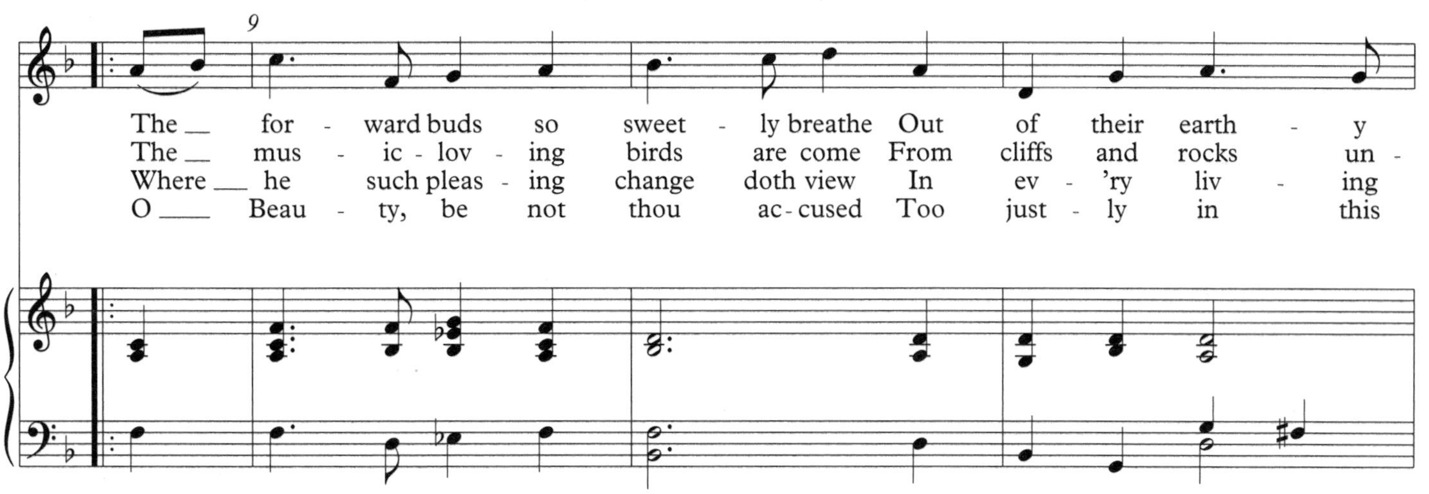
9
The __ for - ward buds so sweet - ly breathe Out of their earth - y
The __ mus - ic - lov - ing birds are come From cliffs and rocks un -
Where __ he such pleas - ing change doth view In ev - ’ry liv - ing
O ___ Beau - ty, be not thou ac - cused Too just - ly in this

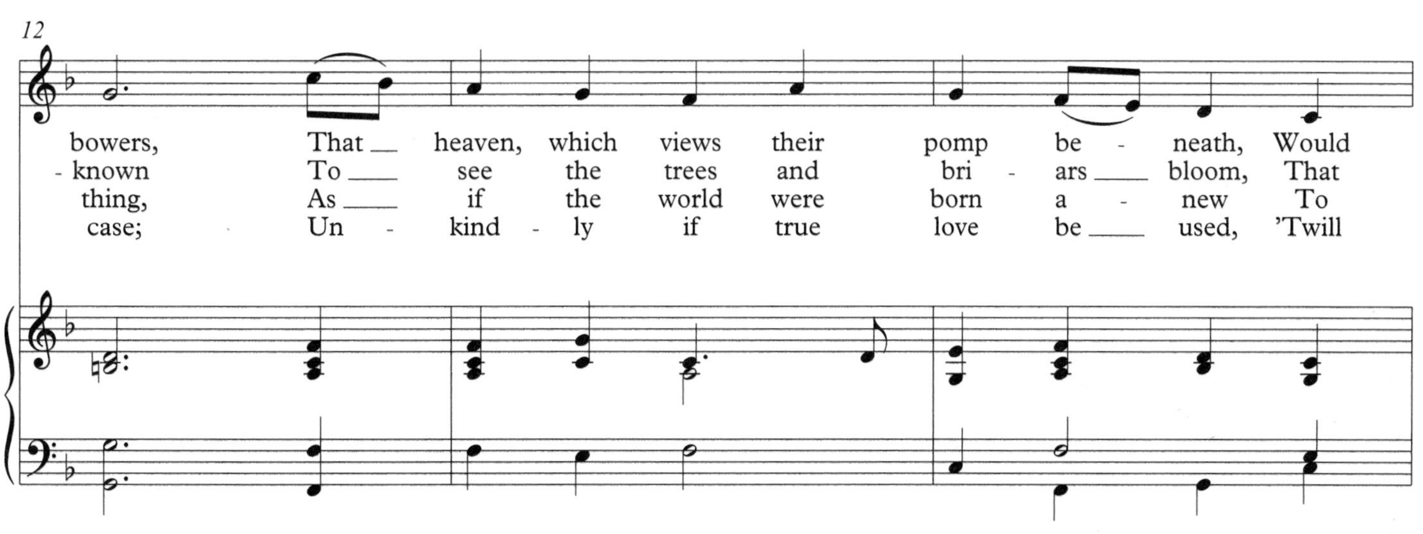
12
bowers, That __ heaven, which views their pomp be - neath, Would
- known To ___ see the trees and bri - ars ___ bloom, That
thing, As ___ if the world were born a - new To
case; Un - kind - ly if true love be ___ used, ’Twill

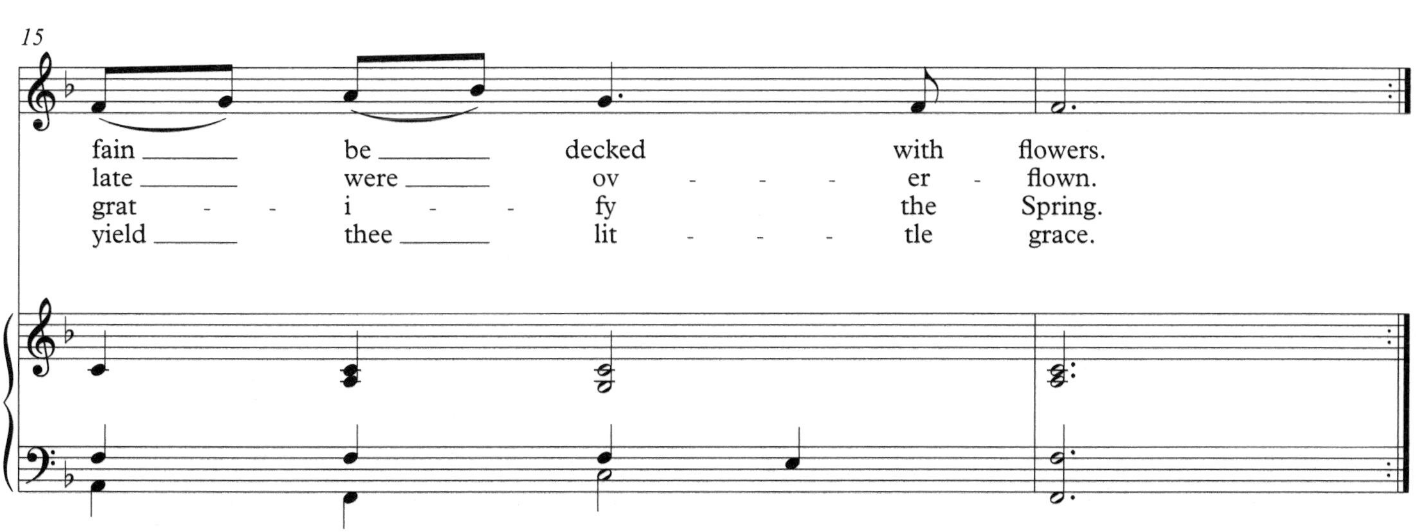
15
fain ______ be ______ decked with flowers.
late ______ were ______ ov - - - - er - flown.
grat - - i - - fy the Spring.
yield ______ thee ______ lit - - - - tle grace.

range:

There is a garden in her face

Thomas Campion (1567–1620) Thomas Campion (1567–1620)

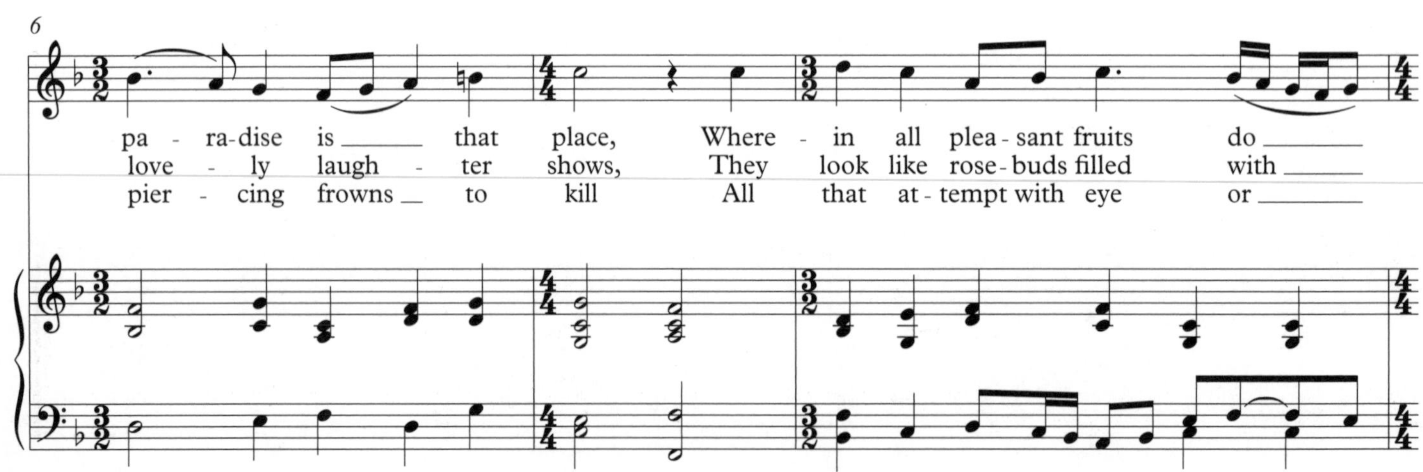

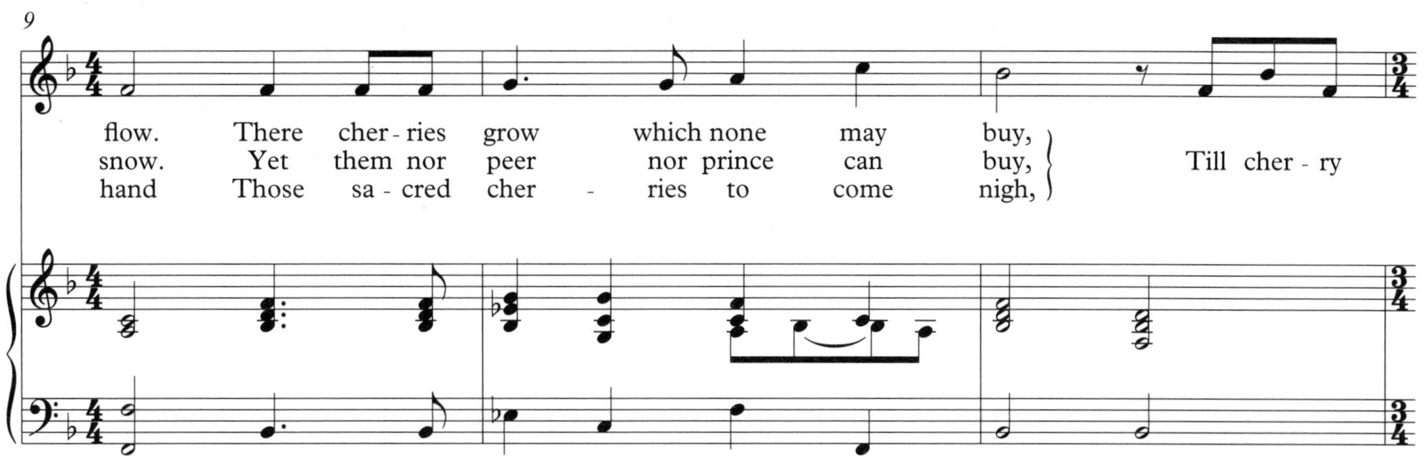
9
flow. There cher-ries grow which none may buy,
snow. Yet them nor peer nor prince can buy,
hand Those sa - cred cher - ries to come nigh,
Till cher - ry

12
ripe, till cher - ry ripe, till cher - ry ripe, cher - ry ripe, ripe,

15
ripe, cher - ry ripe, cher - ry ripe them - selves do cry.

Fair sweet cruel

Thomas Ford (1580–1648)

Thomas Ford (1580–1648)

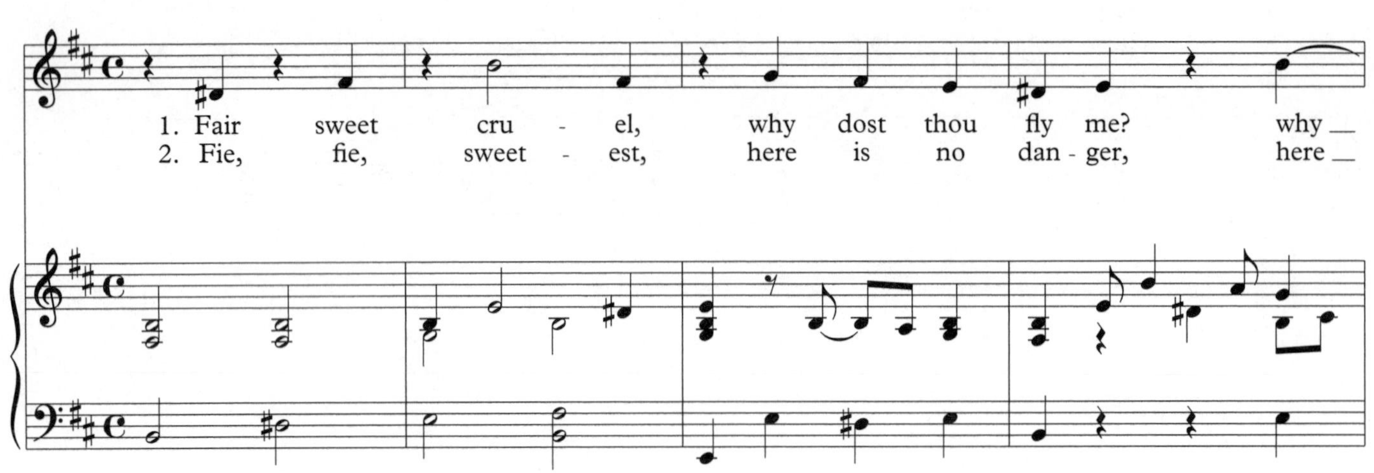

13
then am I near - est.
- er hope re - news me.
Tar-ry then, tar - ry then,

17
O tar-ry, O tar-ry then and take me with you!
Tar-ry then,

22
tar-ry then, O tar-ry, O tar-ry then and take me with you!

range:

Since first I saw your face

Anonymous

Thomas Ford (1580–1648)

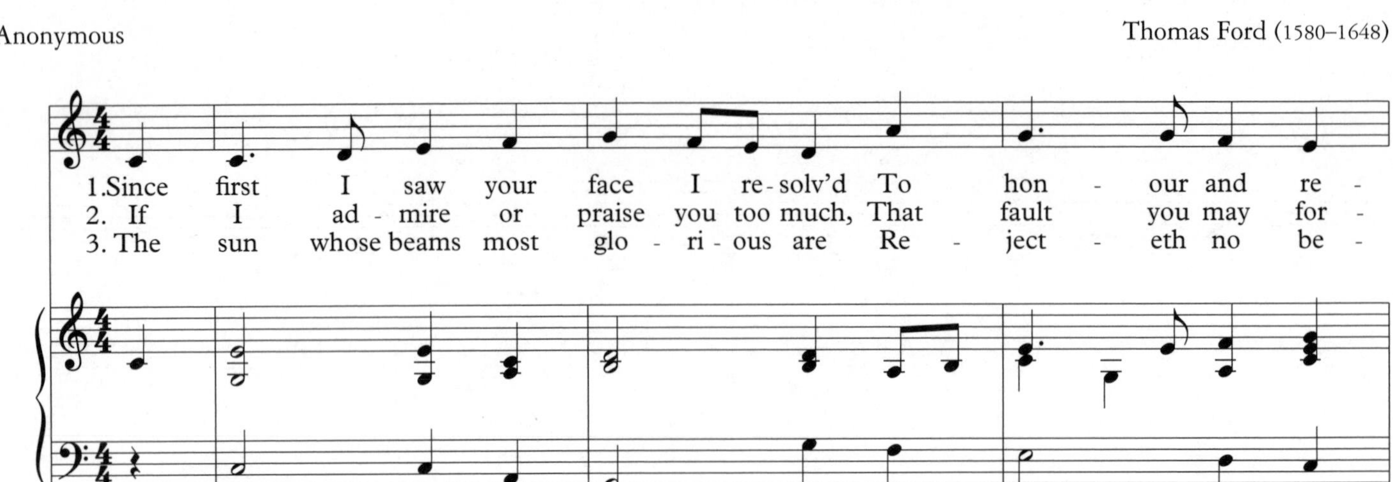

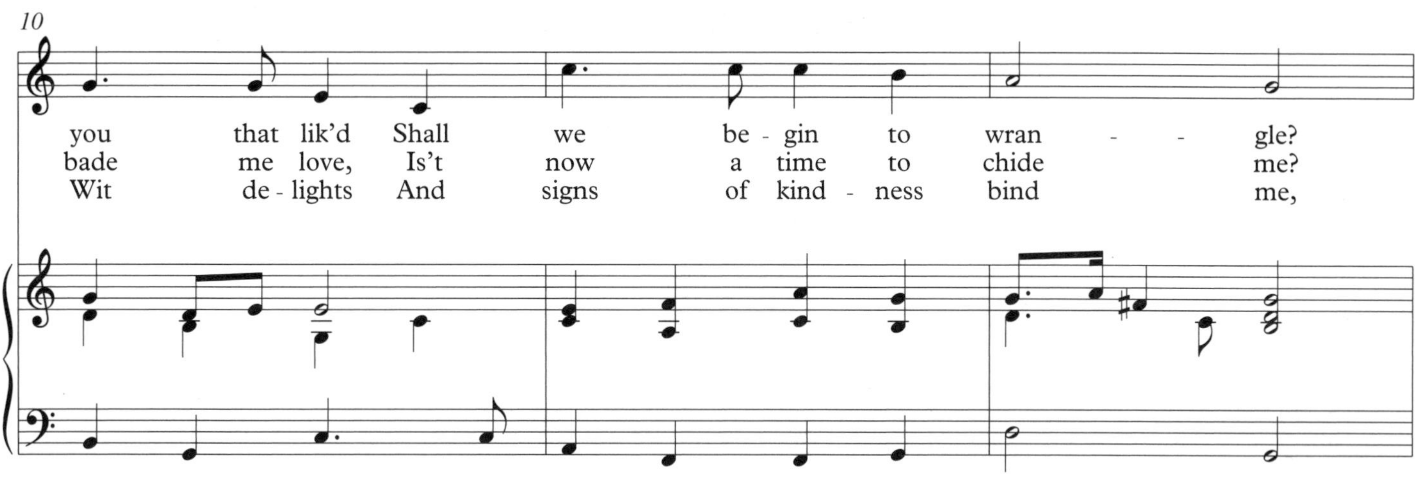
10
you that lik'd Shall we be - gin to wran - - gle?
bade me love, Is't now a time to chide me?
Wit de - lights And signs of kind - ness bind me,

13
No, no, no, my heart is fast, And can - not dis - en - tan - gle.
No, no, no, I'll love you still What for - tune e'er be - tide me.
There, O there, wher-e'er I go, I'll leave my heart be - hind me.

17
No, no, no, my heart is fast, And can - not dis - en - tan - gle.
No, no, no, I'll love you still What for - tune e'er be - tide me.
There, O there, wher-e'er I go, I'll leave my heart be - hind me.

The silver swan

Orlando Gibbons (1583–1625) Orlando Gibbons (1583–1625)

13
last, and sang no more. Fare - well all joys, O
17
death, come close mine eyes. More geese than swans now live, more fools than
21
wise! Fare - well all joys, O death, come close mine
25
eyes. More geese than swans now live, more fools than wise!

range:

I saw my lady weeping

Anonymous

Thomas Morley (1557–1602)

21
But such a woe, be - lieve me, as wins more hearts
24
28
Than mirth can do, than
31
mirth can do with her en - ti - cing parts. parts.
1.
2.

range:

It was a lover and his lass

William Shakespeare (1564–1616) | Thomas Morley (1557–1602)

17
birds do sing hey ding a ding a ding, hey ding a ding a ding, hey ding a ding a ding Sweet
21
lov - ers love the Spring, in Spring time, in Spring time, the
25
on - ly pret - ty ring time, When birds do sing hey ding a ding a ding, hey
29
ding a ding a ding, hey ding a ding a ding, Sweet lov - ers love the Spring.

range:

Ah! how pleasant 'tis to love

John Dryden (1631–1700)

Henry Purcell (1659–1695)

[Allegretto]

range:

I saw that you were grown so high

Anonymous

Henry Purcell (1659–1695)

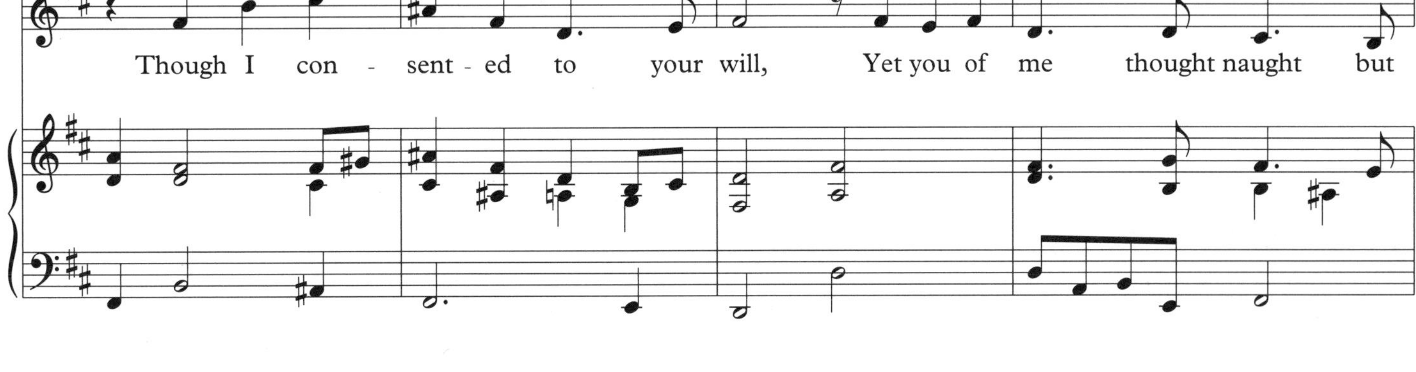

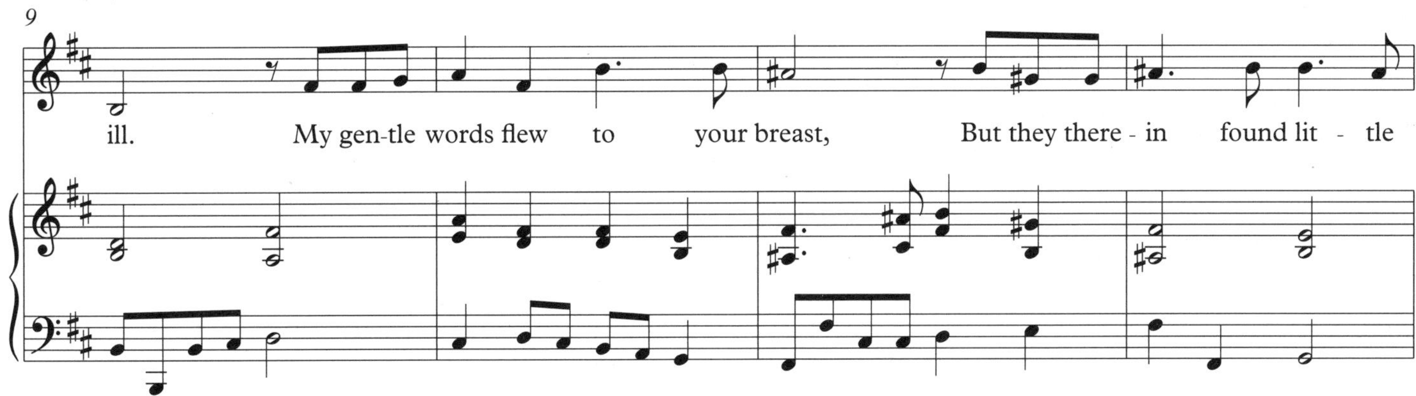

Fairest Isle
(Address to Britain)
from *King Arthur*

range:

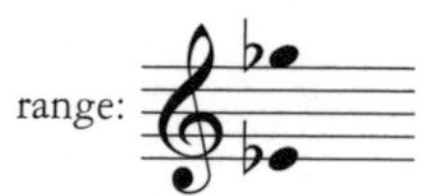

John Dryden (1631–1700)

Henry Purcell (1659–1695)

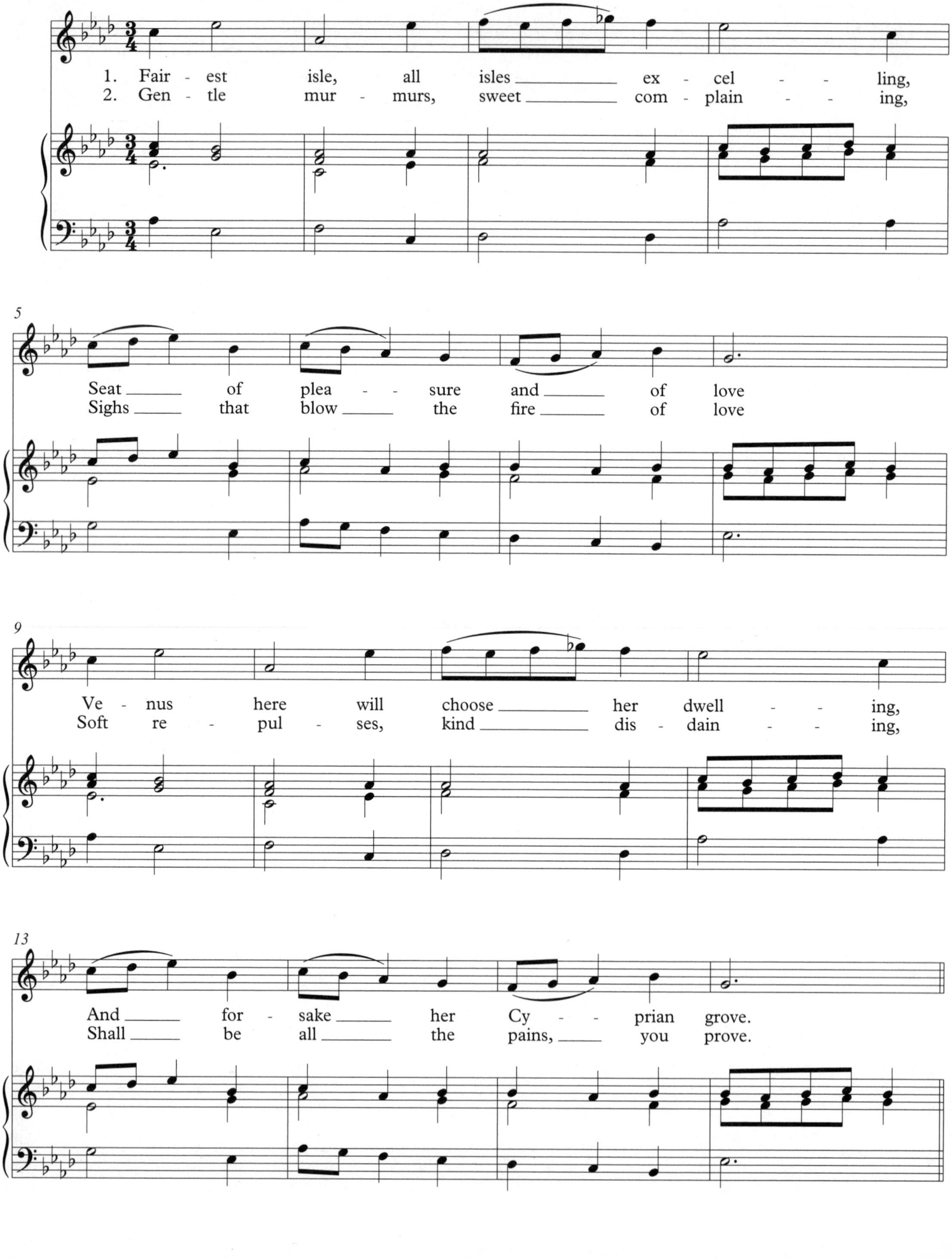
1. Fair - est isle, all isles ___ ex - cel - - ling,
2. Gen - tle mur - murs, sweet ___ com - plain - - ing,
5
Seat ___ of plea - - sure and ___ of love
Sighs ___ that blow ___ the fire ___ of love
9
Ve - nus here will choose ___ her dwell - - ing,
Soft re - pul - ses, kind ___ dis - dain - - ing,
13
And ___ for - sake ___ her Cy - - prian grove.
Shall ___ be all ___ the pains, ___ you prove.

17
Cu - pid from his fav - 'rite na - - tion
Ev - 'ry swain shall pay his du - - ty,

21
Care and en - - vy will re - move;
Grate - - ful ev - - 'ry nymph shall prove;

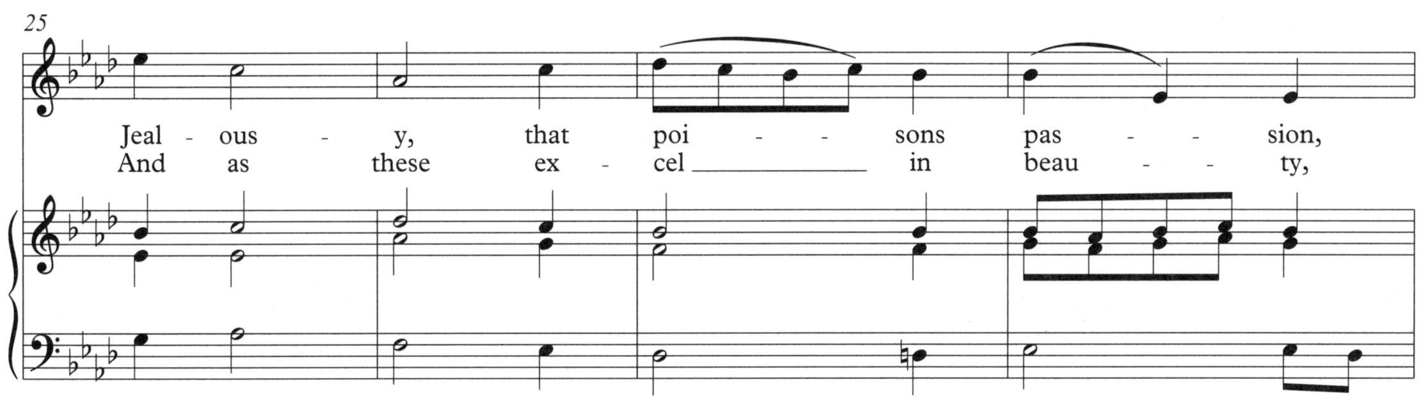
25
Jeal - ous - y, that poi - - sons pas - - sion,
And as these ex - cel in beau - - ty,

29
And des - pair, that dies for love.
Those shall be re - nown'd for love.

If music be the food of love

First Version

Henry Heveningham (1651–1700)

Henry Purcell (1659–1695)

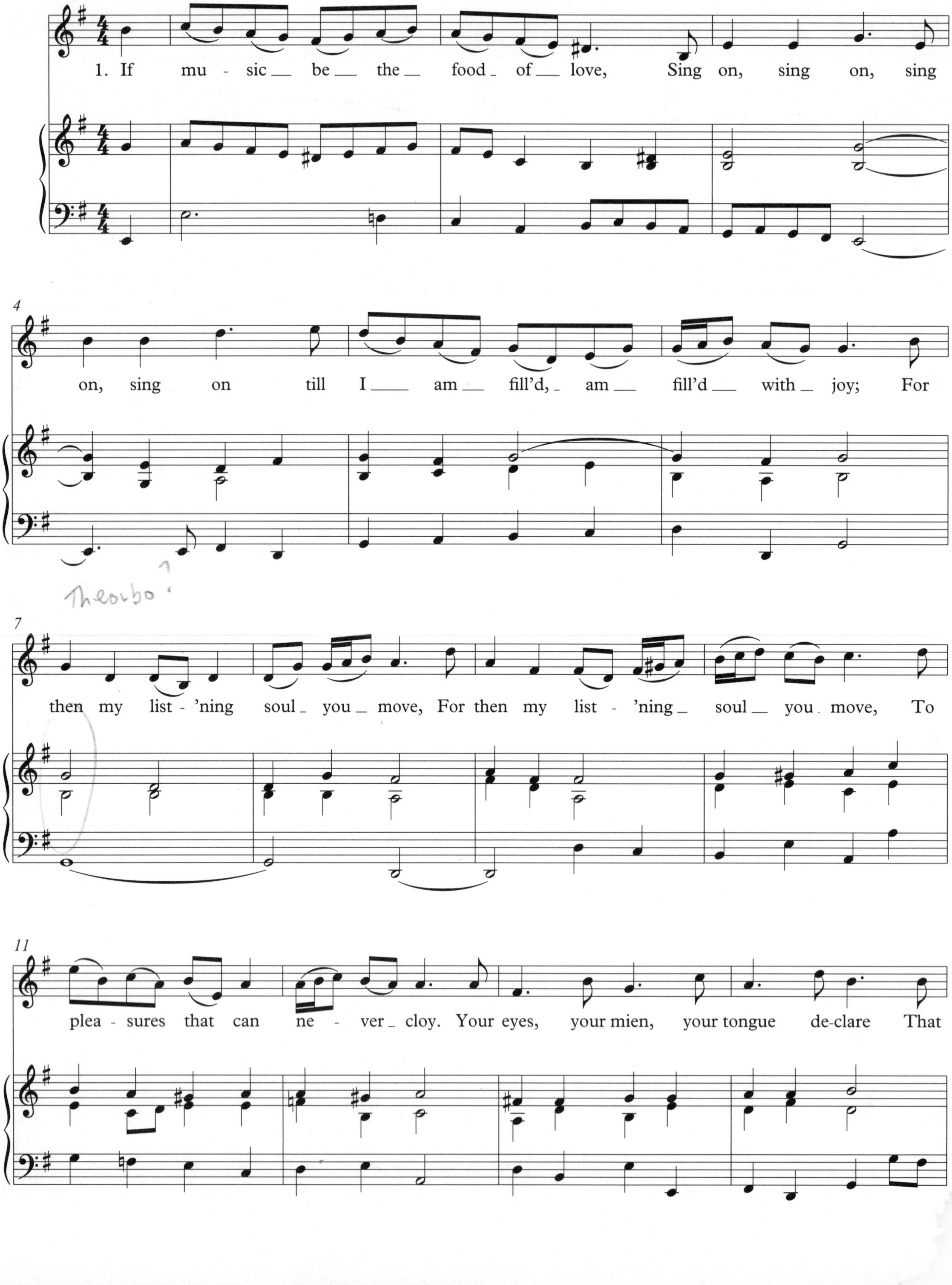

1. If mu - sic be the food of love, Sing on, sing on, sing

4 on, sing on till I am fill'd, am fill'd with joy; For

7 then my list - 'ning soul you move, For then my list - 'ning soul you move, To

11 plea - sures that can ne - ver cloy. Your eyes, your mien, your tongue de-clare That

15
you are mu - - sic ev - 'ry - where, Your eyes, your mien, your
19
tongue de-clare That you are mu - - sic ev - 'ry - where.
23
2. Plea - sures in - vade both eye and ear, So fierce, so fierce, so
26
fierce, so fierce, the trans - - - - ports are, they wound, And

29
all my sen - ses feast - ed __ are, And all my sen - ses __ feast - ed __ are; Tho'
33
yet __ the __ treat _ is on - ly __ sound, Sure I must per - ish by your charms, Un -
37
- less you save __ me _ in your _ arms, Sure I must per - ish
41
by your charms, Un - less you save __ me __ in your _ arms.

range: 

Man is for the woman made

from *The Mock Marriage*

Peter Anthony Motteux (1663–1718)

Henry Purcell (1659–1695)

Man, man, man is for the woman made, And the woman made for man.

1. As the spur is for the jade, As the scab-bard for the blade, As for dig-ging is the spade, As for li-quor is the can,
2. As the scep-tre to be sway'd, As for night's the se-re-nade, As for pud-ding is the pan, And to cool us is the fan,
3. Be she wi-dow, be she maid, Be she wan-ton, be she staid, Be she well or ill ar-ray'd, Que-an, slut, or har-ri-dan,

So man, man, man is for the woman made, And the woman for the man.

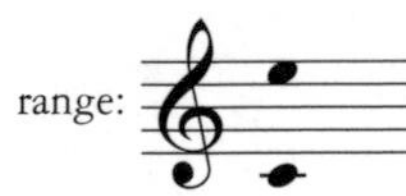

range:

Love quickly is pall'd

Thomas Shadwell (1640–1692)

Henry Purcell (1659–1695)

[Vivace]

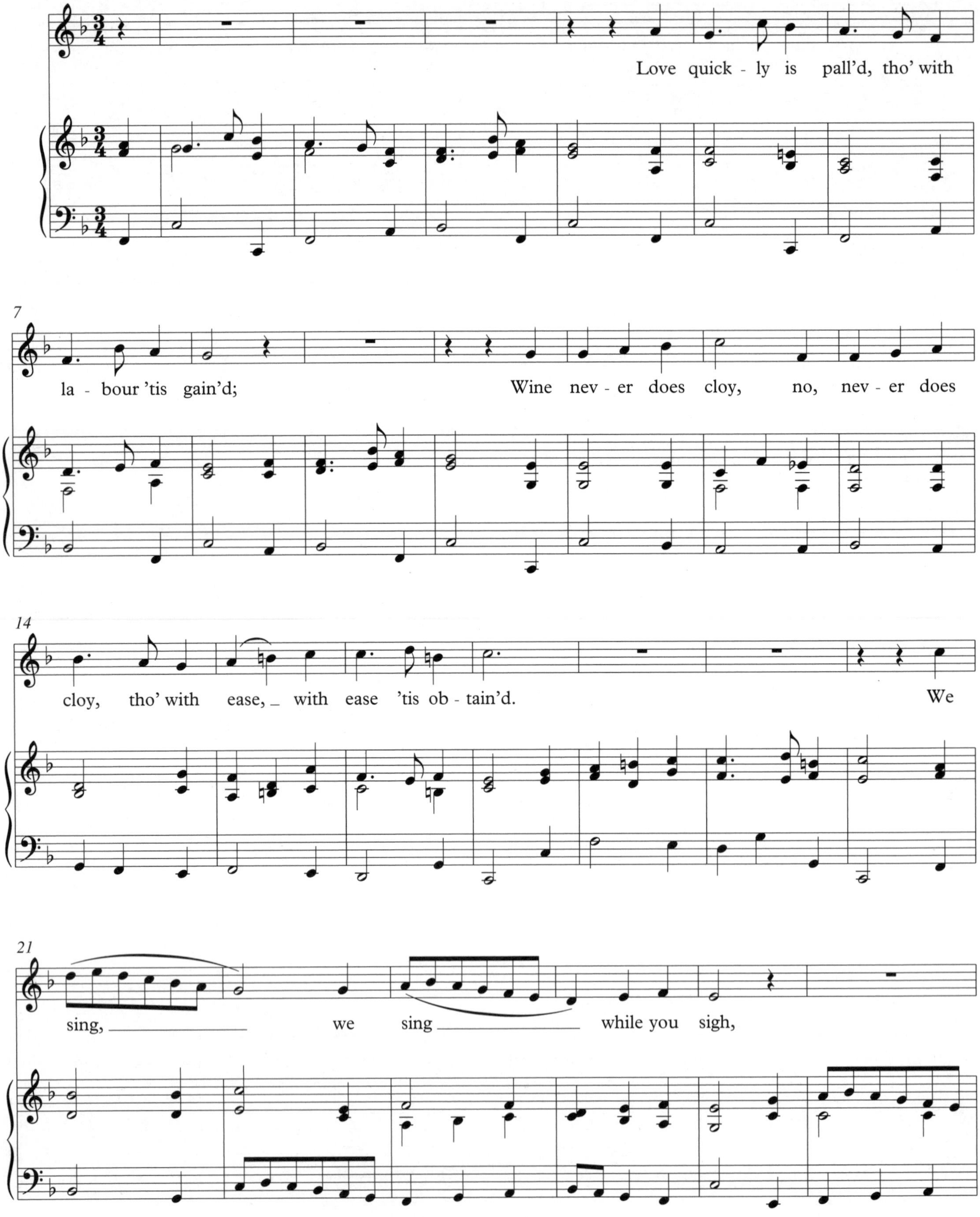
Love quick - ly is pall'd, tho' with
7
la - bour 'tis gain'd; Wine nev - er does cloy, no, nev - er does
14
cloy, tho' with ease, _ with ease 'tis ob - tain'd. We
21
sing, we sing while you sigh,

27
we laugh, we laugh, we laugh, laugh while you
33
weep; Love robs you of rest, love
41
robs you of rest, Wine lulls us, lulls us, lulls us, lulls us,
49
lulls us a - sleep.

range: 

Music for a while

John Dryden (1631–1700)

Henry Purcell (1659–1695)

Mu - sic,

5

mu - - sic for _ a _ while Shall all your cares _ be - quile, _ shall all, all,

8

all, shall all, shall all ___ shall all _ your cares be - guile: _ Won -

11

- d'ring, won - - d'ring how your pains ___ were eas'd, ___ eas'd, ___

14
eas'd And dis - dain-ing to be pleas'd, Till A - lec - to free the -
17
dead, till A - lec - - to free the dead From their e - ter - - -
20
- nal, e - ter - - - - - nal bands,
23
Till the snakes drop, drop, drop, drop, drop, drop, drop, drop, drop,

26
from ___ her head And the whip, and the whip from out her_ hands.
29
Mu - sic, mu - - sic for _ a __ while Shall all your cares _ be -
32
- guile, _ shall all, all, all, shall all, all, all, ___ shall all _ your cares be -
35
- guile, all, all, all, all, all, all, all, all, shall all _ your cares be - guile.

Since from my dear

from *Dioclesian*

Thomas Betterton (1635–1710)

Henry Purcell (1659–1695)

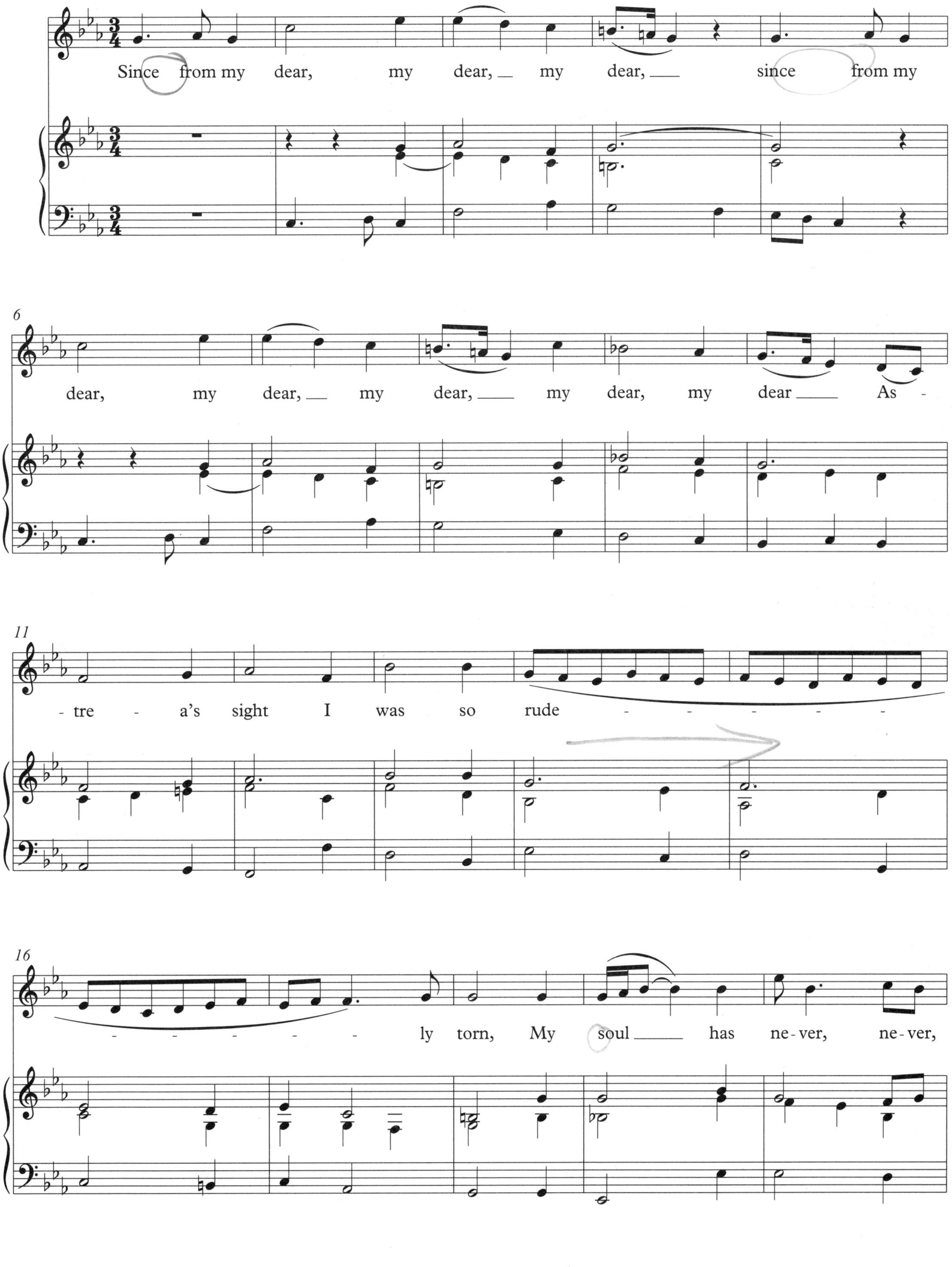

Since from my dear, my dear, — my dear, — since from my

6 dear, my dear, — my dear, — my dear, my dear — As -

11 - tre - a's sight I was so rude - - - - - -

16 - - - - - ly torn, My soul — has ne-ver, ne-ver,

21
ne - ver, has ne - ver, ne - ver, ne - ver known de - light, Un - less it
26
were to mourn, to mourn, un - less, un -
No Repeat
31
1.
2.
- less it were to mourn, mourn. But oh! a -
35
- las, a - las, with weep - ing eyes. And bleed - ing,

40
bleed - ing heart I lie; Think - ing on her, on
45
her, whose ab - sence 'tis, That makes me wish to
50
die, die, die, die, makes me,
55
makes me wish to die, die, die.

Nymphs and shepherds

range:

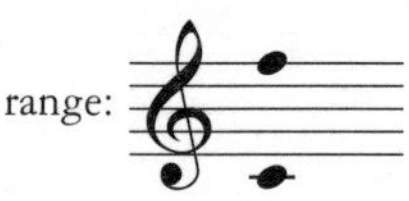

from *The Libertine*

Thomas Shadwell (1642–1692)

Henry Purcell (1659–1695)

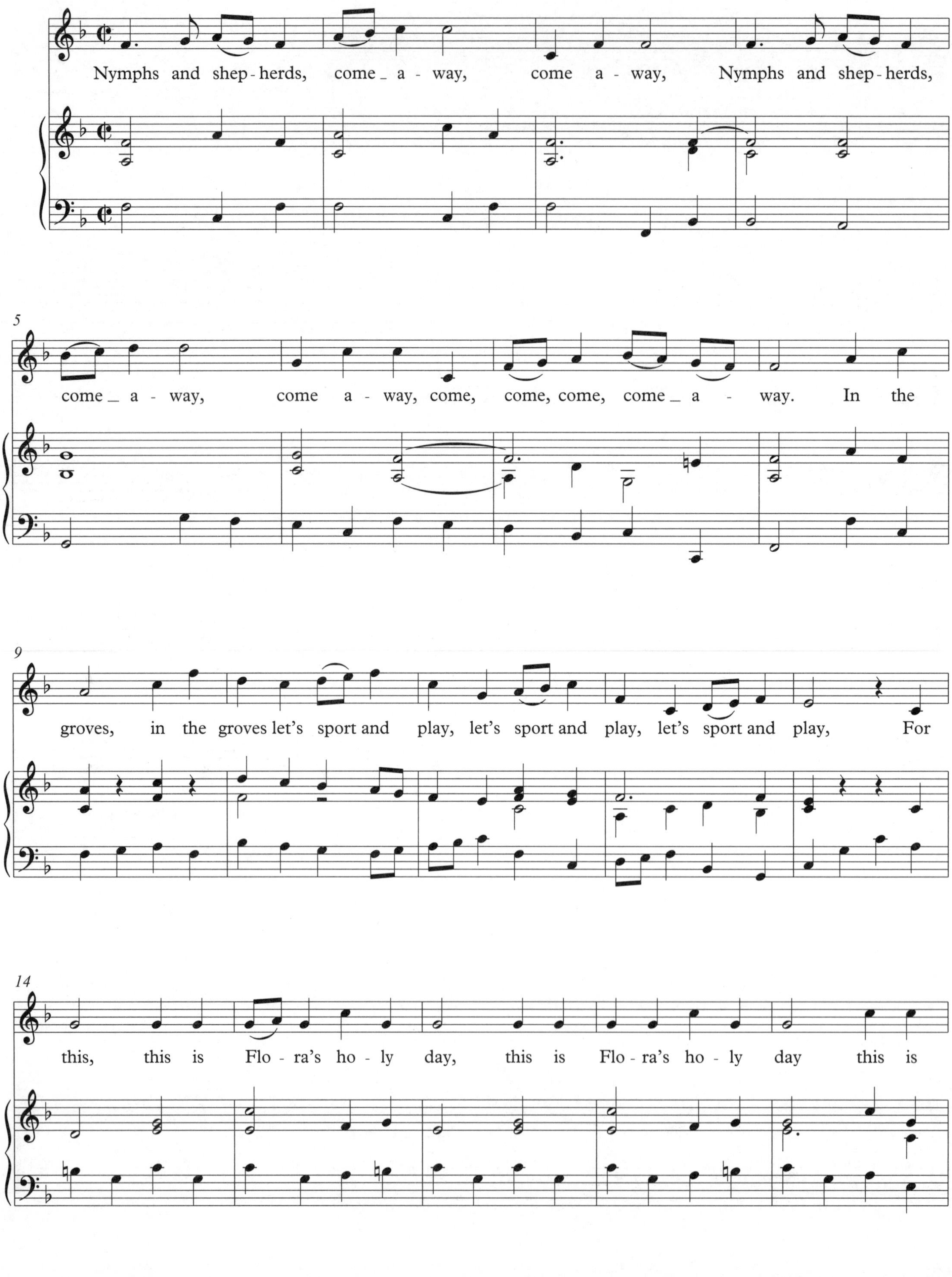
Nymphs and shep-herds, come _ a - way, come a - way, Nymphs and shep-herds,
5
come _ a - way, come a - way, come, come, come, come _ a - way. In the
9
groves, in the groves let's sport and play, let's sport and play, let's sport and play, For
14
this, this is Flo - ra's ho - ly day, this is Flo - ra's ho - ly day this is

19
p
Flo - ra's ho - ly day, Sa - cred to ease
24
and hap - py love, To danc - ing, to mu - - - - sic, to
29
danc - ing, to mu - - - - - - sic and to
33
po - e - try; Your flocks may now, now, now, now, now, now, now, now, now,

38
now se - cure - ly rove
Whilst you ex - press, whilst
42
you ex - press
your
46
jol - li - ty.
Nymphs and Shep-herds, come a - way,
51
come a - way, Nymphs and Shep-herds, come a - way,
come a - way, come, come, come, come a - way.

Turn then thine eyes

Elkanah Settle (1648–1724)

Henry Purcell (1659–1695)

9
1.
2.
f
glo - - - - ries there, there. And

11
p
catch-ing, catch-ing flames, catch-ing, catch-ing flames

14
f
p
will on thy, on thy torch ap - pear, and catch-ing, catch-ing flames, and
f
p

17
f
catch-ing, catch-ing flames,
catch-ing, catch-ing flames
will
f

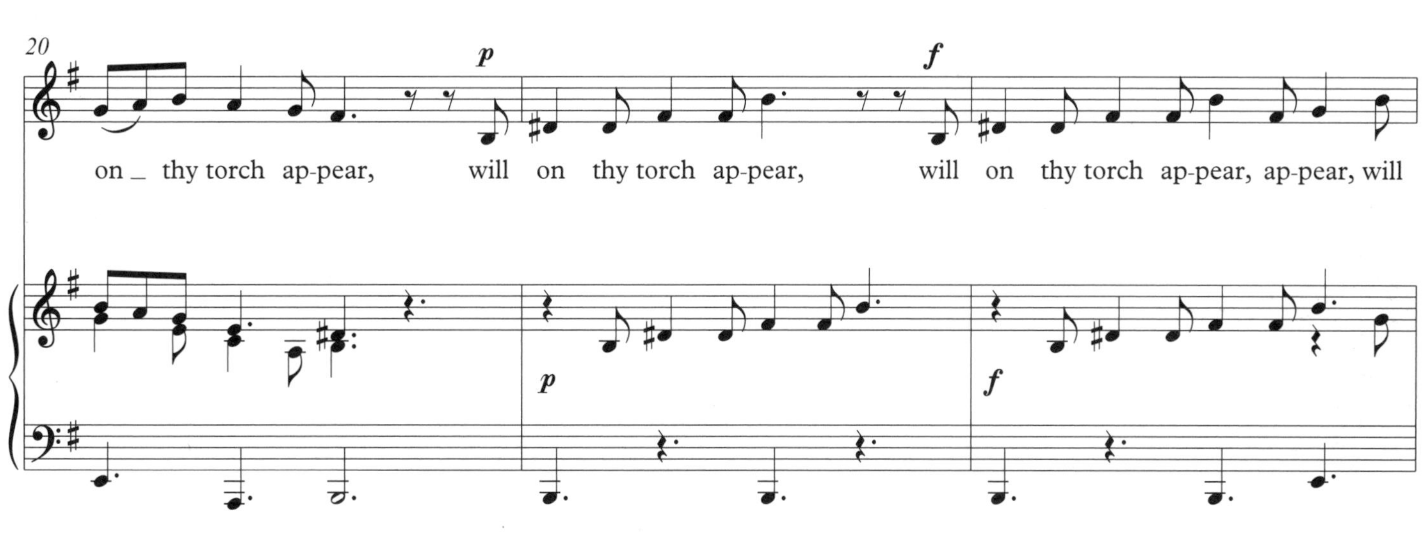
20
p
f
on _ thy torch ap-pear,
will on thy torch ap-pear,
will on thy torch ap-pear, ap-pear, will
p
f

23
p
1.
f
2.
on _ thy torch ap-pear
will on _ thy torch ap-pear
And on _ thy torch ap - pear.
p
f

What shall I do

from *Dioclesian*

Thomas Betterton (1635–1710)

Henry Purcell (1659–1695)

1. What shall I do to show how much I love her?
2. Since gods them - selves could not ev - er be lov - ing,

5
How ma - ny mil - lions of sighs can suf - fice?
Men must have breath - ing re - cruits for new joys;

9
That which wins oth - er's hearts, ne - ver can move her,
I wish my love could be ev - er im - prov - ing,

13
Those com - mon me - thods of love she'll des - pise.
Though ea - ger love more than sor - row des - troys.

17
I will love more than man e'er lov'd before me;
In fair Au - re - lia's arms leave me ex - pir - - - ing,

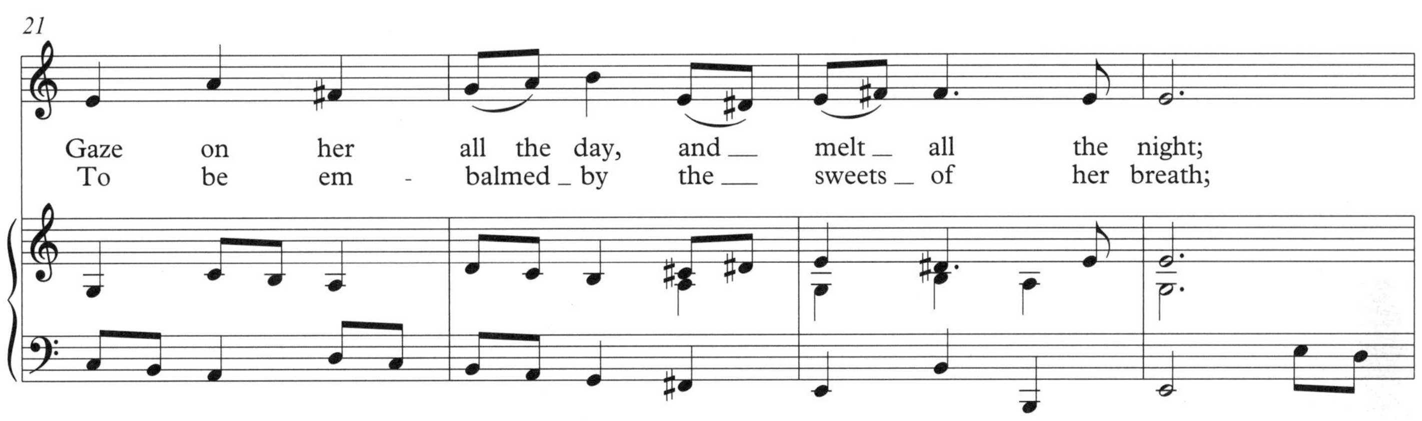
21
Gaze on her all the day, and melt all the night;
To be em - balmed by the sweets of her breath;

25
'Till for her own sake at last she'll im - plore me,
To the last mo - ment I'll still ne de - sir - - - ing;

29
D.C.
To love her less, to pre - serve our de - light.
Ne - ver had he - ro so glo - rious a death.

When I am laid in earth
(*Dido's Lament*)

Nahum Tate (1652–1715)

Henry Purcell (1659–1695)

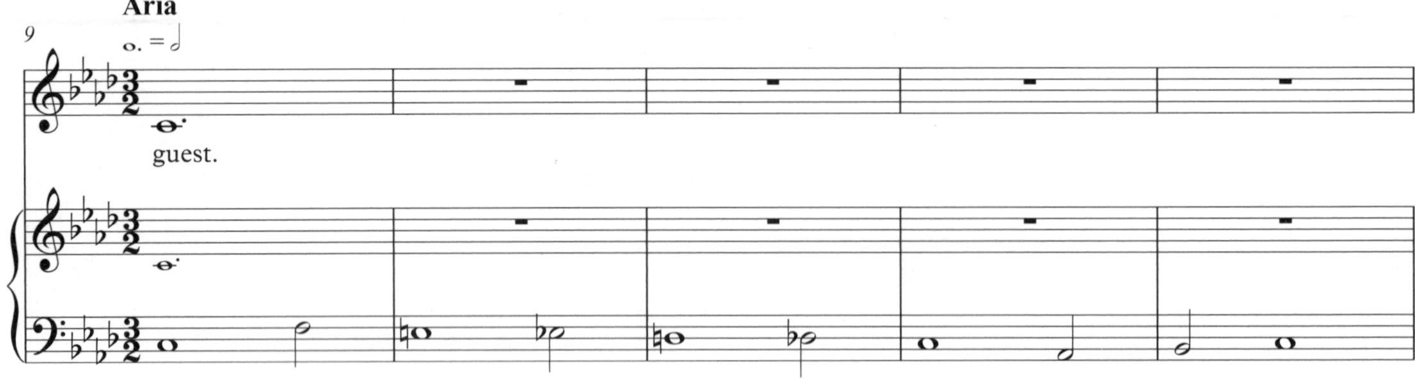

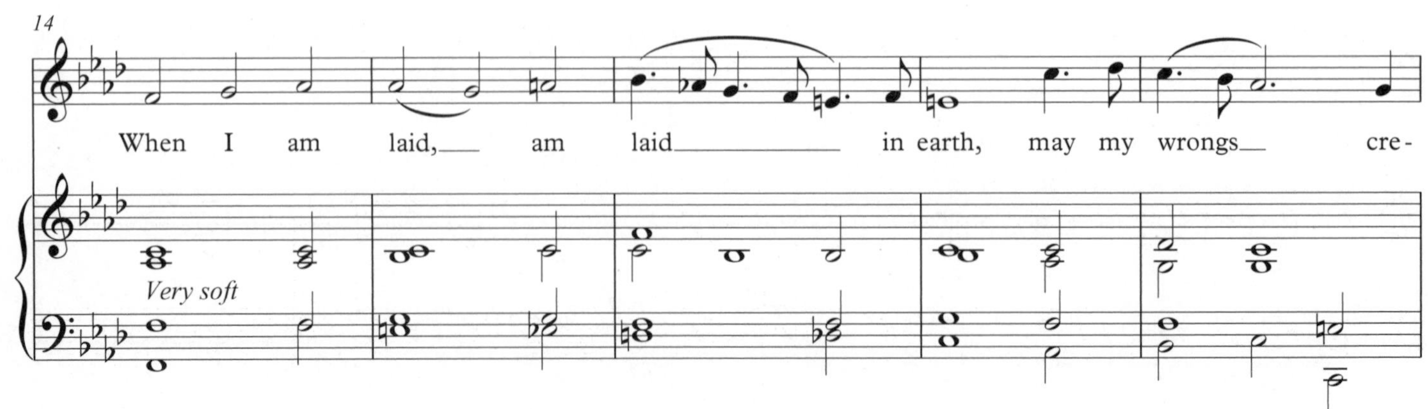

19
-ate no trou - ble, no trou-ble in thy breast.

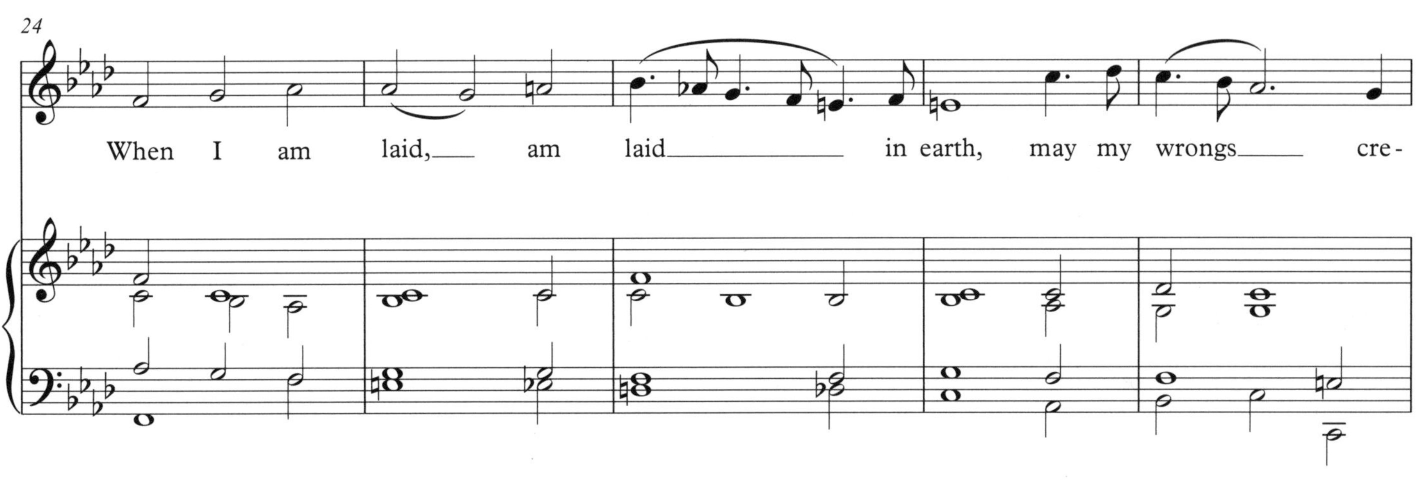
24
When I am laid, am laid in earth, may my wrongs cre-

29
-ate no trou - ble, no trou-ble in thy breast. Re-

34
-mem - ber me, re - mem - ber me, but ah!

39
for-get my fate, re - mem - ber me, but ah! for - get my

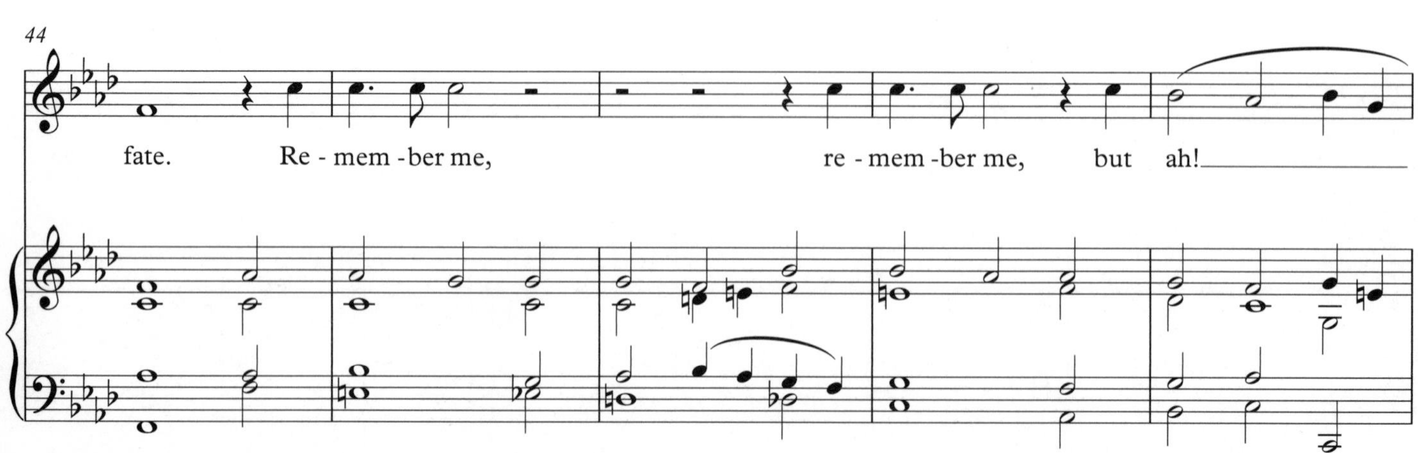
44
fate. Re - mem - ber me, re - mem - ber me, but ah!

49

54

59

range: 

The Knotting Song

Sir Charles Sedley (1639–1701)

Henry Purcell (1659–1695)

[Allegretto]

1. "Hears not my Phil - lis how the birds, Their feath - er'd mates sa - lute? They tell their pas - sion in their words, Must I a - lone, must I a - lone be mute?"
2. "The God of love in thy bright eyes Does like a ty - rant reign; But in thy heart a child he lies, With - out his dart, with - out his dart or flame."
3. "So ma - ny months in si - lence past, And yet in rag - ing love, Might well de - serve one word at last, My pas - sion, my pas - sion should ap - prove."
4. "Must then your faith - ful swain ex - pire, and not one look ob - tain, Which he to soothe his fond de - sire, Might pleas - ing - ly, might pleas - ing - ly ex - plain?"

Phil - lis, with - out a frown or smile, Sat and knot-ted, and knot-ted, and knot-ted, and knot - ted all the while.

When Laura smiles

Thomas Campion (1567–1620)

Philip Rosseter (1567/8–1623)

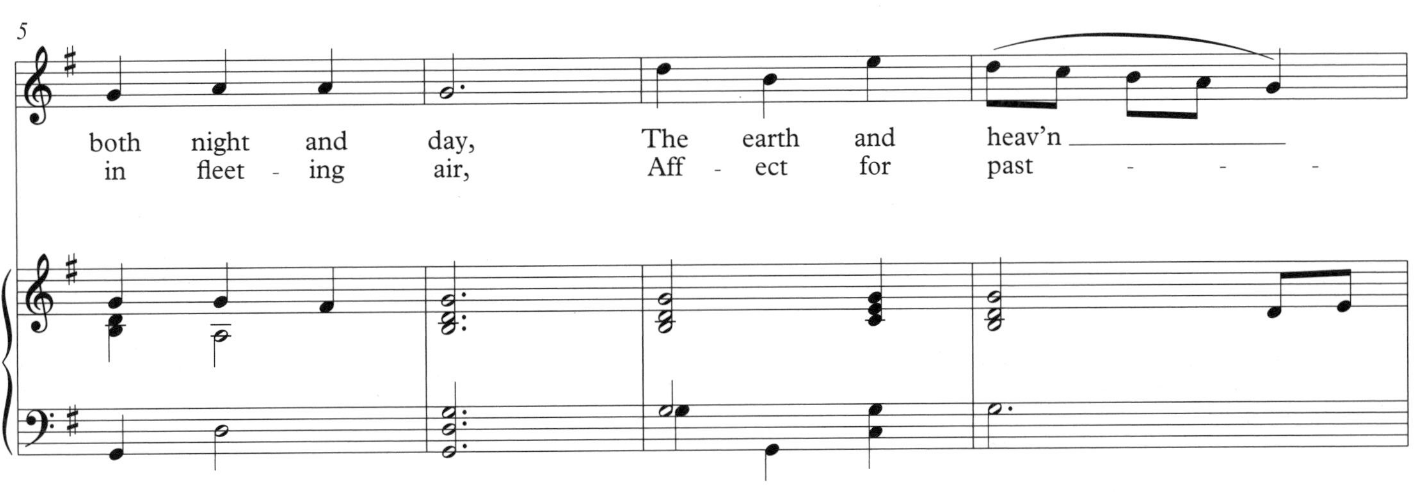

13
And her speech with ev - er - flow - ing mu - sic doth re - pair, The
And the birds think sweet Au - ro - ra Mor - ning's queen doth shine, From

19
D.C.
cru - el wounds of sor - row and un - tam'd des - pair.
her bright sphere when Lau - ra shows her looks di - vine.

24
3. Di - a - na's eyes are not a - dorn'd
4. Love hath no fire but what he steals

28
with grea - ter pow'r Than Lau - ra's when
from her bright eyes, Time hath no pow'r
32
she lists a - while for sport to lour
but that which in her plea - sure lies,
36
But when she her eyes en - clo - seth, blind - ness doth ap - pear, The
For she with her di - vine beau - ties all the world sub - dues, And
42
D.S.
chief - est grace of beau - ty sweet - - ly seat - ed there.
fills with heav'n - ly spi - - rits my hum - ble Muse.

If she forsake me

Anonymous

Philip Rosseter (1567/8–1623)

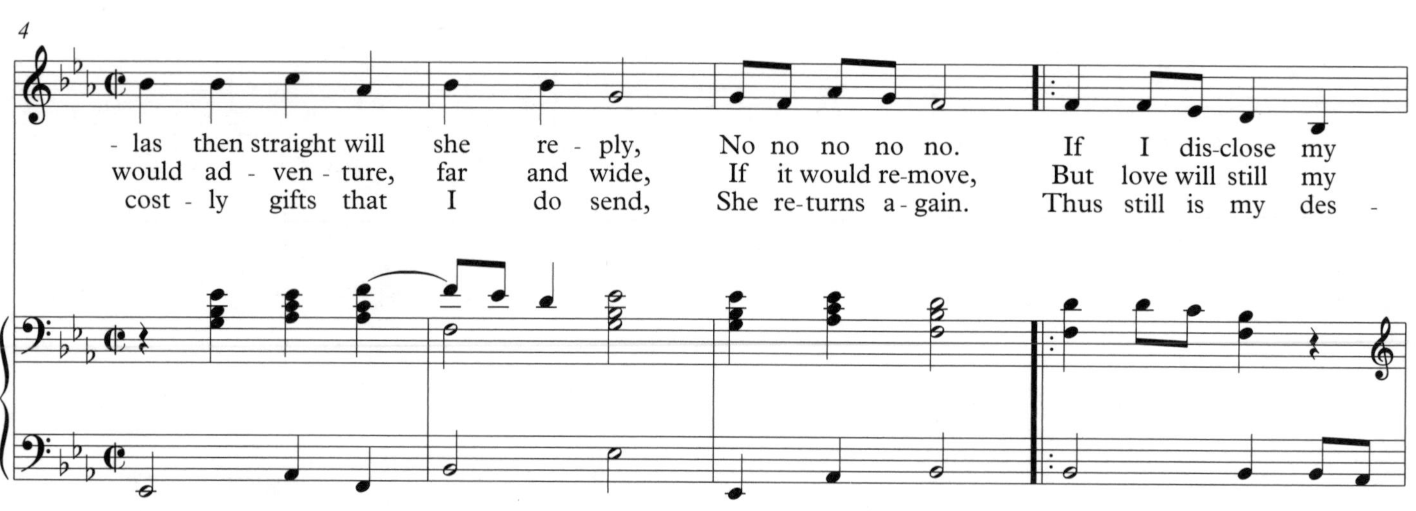

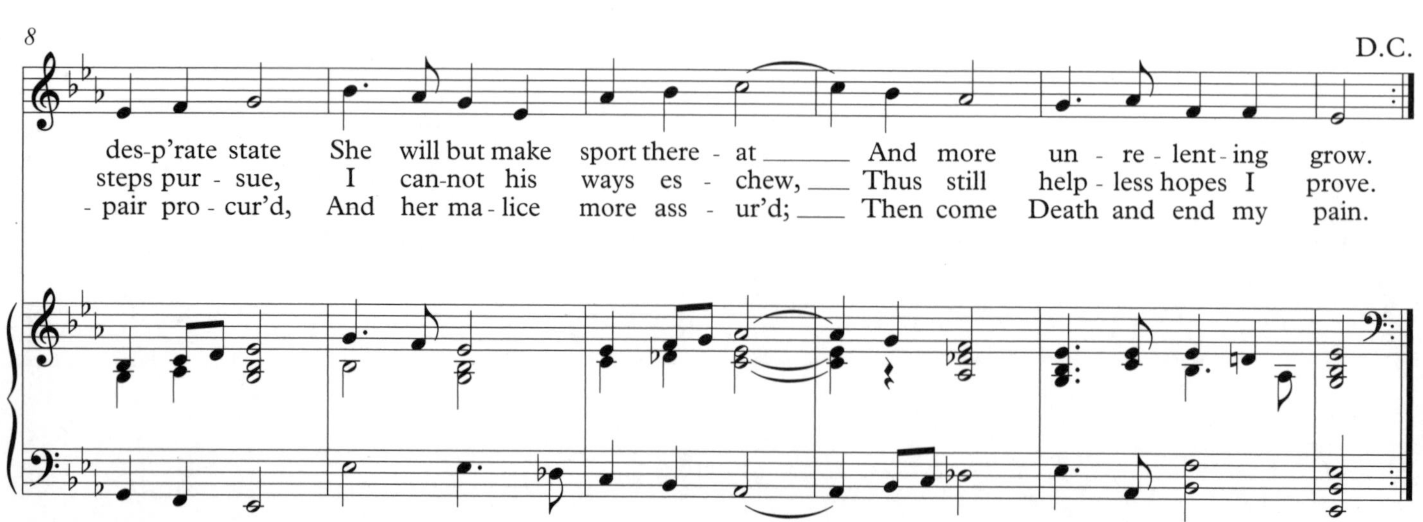